Professional WORKBOOK

START

Lead Well • **Be Well** • Do Well

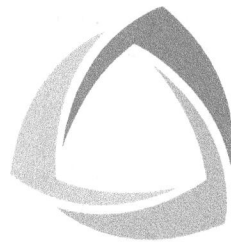

**Develop the mindset and skills you need
to lead in a highly competitive world**

Laurie Bodine

Well Well Well Press

The following are Trademarks and/or Copyrights of START Leadership:

The Business & Family Organization	WIN Map
The Complete Leader	START Leadership Process
RRR: Leadership Attributes	Essential Leadership Skills

Publisher's Note: This publication is designed to provide information only in regard to the subject matter covered. It is not intended to provide psychological or professional services.

Published by Well Well Well Press, San Francisco, CA

Cover design by Melissa Hutton

Library of Congress/ISBN 978-0-9883599-5-6

Printed in the United States of America

Author's Website: START-Leadership.com

CONTENTS

INTRODUCTION
Take the Lead

Everyone is born with the capacity to lead. In fact, research proves that leadership can be learned, practiced, and mastered by anyone. From taking the lead in your own life to taking the lead on your projects, teams, and in your work, everyone is in a position to take the lead and to lead well. The best news for those who lead well is that it's proven to deliver greater well being, happiness, and success for you and often, for your colleagues.

Here's why: When we analyze and synthesize the research, three related themes emerge.

1. Happiness drives success (not the other way around)
   When we are well, we can do well.
2. Leadership drives happiness
   When we develop mastery, autonomy, and purpose, we thrive.
3. START drives leadership
   When we practice leadership language and processes, we build essential know-how for leading and living life well.

In this workbook, these three themes are embedded into a straightforward framework that you can use to lead well in your own life at work, at home, and in your community.

The concepts, reflections, and worksheets in this workbook provide the tools you need to explore and connect

- *who you are at your best* and how that aligns with
- *what you care about most* so you can
- *take the lead in making a difference*
- *in ways that are meaningful to you* and
- *that have value in the world.*

Those who practice this leadership approach report greater satisfaction, engagement, and enjoyment, even in the midst of working hard and facing the inevitable challenges of work and life. As you put these tools to work for yourself, you'll find you're able to develop the mindset and skills that are essential to achieving success and happiness in today's highly competitive and rapidly changing world.

You have everything you need. START Now.

Part One
The START Leader

In this section, you'll find a couple of working definitions for leadership, including informal and formal leadership, and the tools that contribute to optimizing your leadership mindset:

WIN Map Summary: A tool to introduce the relationship between innate **W**iring, your **I**nterests, and **N**eeds you can address in the world

Wiring & Individual Assessments:

- **Strengths Summary and Reflection:** A tool for you to *identify the situations and factors that support the use of your strengths most effectively*

- **EQ Summary and Reflection:** A tool for you to *Emotional Intelligence (EQ) in order to maximize the positive and minimize the negative*

- **Complete Leadership Style Summary and Reflection:** A tool for you to *identify the situations and factors that support the alignment and use of appropriate leadership styles*

WIN Map Reflection Worksheet: A tool for you to map your innate Wiring to address Needs you discover in areas that are of Interest to you

Leadership Definitions

Leadership can be defined broadly, from both a small "l" leadership and Big "L" Leadership perspective. Using consistent language that describes the actions and interactions you have on a regular basis provides an opportunity to connect to and develop leadership opportunities in your life.

Small "l" leadership: Leading Self
Make decisions and take actions that have positive and productive outcomes.

Big "L" Leadership: Leading Others
Mobilize yourself and others in pursuit of worthwhile goals.

Small "l" leadership is the day-to-day leadership and initiative you demonstrate when you make decisions and take actions that have positive and productive outcomes.

Examples of small "l" leadership:

- Arriving on time for meetings
- Doing what you say you will do when you say you will do it
- Effectively communicating with those who depend on your input
- Acting with integrity, even when doing so is hard
- Holding the door for someone, picking up trash on the sidewalk, volunteering in the community, voting in civic elections

Big "L" Leadership is the goal-directed leadership that you demonstrate when you work alone or with others to achieve worthwhile goals—whether you are in a position of authority or not. Big "L" Leadership is about understanding what needs to be done, why your participation is important, and how you can mobilize yourself and others to get the work done well.

Examples of Big "L" Leadership:

- Managing and leading a project team or department that works well together and meets objectives on time and on budget
- Planning and organizing activities that serve others such as volunteering in the community
- Engaging in a mission-driven organization as a founder, officer, or member

The WIN Map Summary

When you use the way you're innately **W**ired to address **N**eeds in areas that are of **I**nterest, you engage and excel naturally. In this process, you will increasingly experience a connection to the purpose of your work that will engage you and allow you to map your path as you make decisions about your career. This WIN Map will continue to serve you throughout your life—personally, and professionally. It's true for everyone: when we align what we're good at with what we like and apply both to address needs at work, in your family, and in your community, we're at our best and can maximize our value and contribution. Use the WIN Map to:

- Tune into and assess how you are innately **W**ired—the natural strengths, talents, and skills you use to approach situations and people around you. Assessing your Emotional Intelligence and your Leadership Style also provides insight in maximizing the effectiveness of the way you're naturally Wired.
- Tune into and assess your **I**nterests—identify the things that you like, like to do, and/or care about.
- Tune into and assess the **N**eeds you discover in the world in your family, community, and work.

The WIN Map
Individual Discovery and Connection

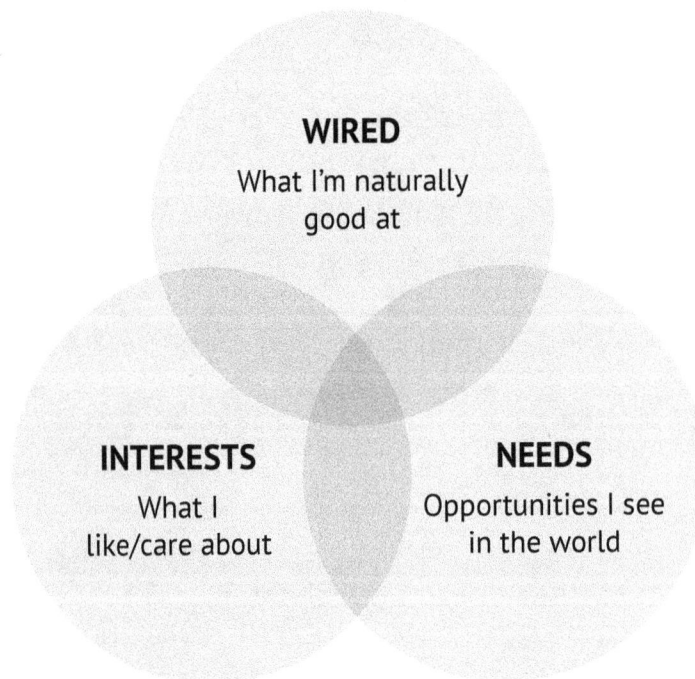

WIRED
What I'm naturally
good at

INTERESTS
What I
like/care about

NEEDS
Opportunities I see
in the world

= **Path to Performance, Engagement, and Satisfaction**

Wired: **Strengths** Summary

Best and Stressed   When we're at our best, the way we're naturally wired contributes to our ability to do productive work and to interact well with others. When we invest in and develop what comes most naturally to us, we can turn our innate predispositions into strengths.

When we're under stress, our strengths can be unproductive and can actually interfere with our work and interactions with others. We become more effective both personally and professionally when we maximize times we're at our best, and understand and manage our tendencies when we are stressed.

Reflecting on how and when we use our strengths helps us to maximize times we're at our best.

natural
abilities
Strengths
gifts
Qualities
core talents

1. Self Reflection

Identify your top 5 strengths—areas in which you naturally excel. Strengths assessment resources are listed in the bibliography. Describe an example of how each of your strengths help you to be more effective professionally and personally.

Strength 1:

Strength 2:

Strength 3:

Strength 4:

Strength 5:

2. Situational Reflection

Best: Contributors

1. Describe a time you used a strength effectively in a challenging situation.

2. Consider the factors that may have contributed to your effectiveness.
   - Ample Time
   - Well Prepared
   - Clear Objectives
   - Calm
   - Collaborative
   - Other _____

Stressed: Triggers

1. Describe a time you used a strength that was ineffective in a challenging situation.

2. Consider the factors that may have triggered your lack of effectiveness.
   - Time Crunched
   - Ill Prepared
   - Lack of Desired Control
   - Unclear Objectives
   - Worried
   - Other _____

3. Taking Action

Identify 2 or 3 things you can do to maximize your Best behavior and minimize your Stressed behavior.

1.

2.

3.

START
Lead Well • Be Well • Do Well

9

Notes:

Wired: EQ Summary

Best and Stressed   Comprehensive research shows that emotional intelligence (EQ) is the single most effective predictor of leadership effectiveness and overall success—beating both IQ and technical competence. Developing high EQ prepares us to better deal with the strong or unexpected emotions that can hijack our rational thinking and interfere with productive actions and interactions.

Strengthening our EQ in four key areas can help us act most effectively, even in difficult situations. These four areas include two in knowledge: self-awareness and awareness of others; and two in behavior: self-management and relationship management.

Reflecting on the situations and factors that impact our own EQ is the first step in raising our EQ.

EQ: Emotional Intelligence

	What I See	What I Do
Personal	**Self-Awareness**	**Self-Management**
Social	**Social-Awareness**	**Relationship-Management**

11

1. Self Reflection

Self-Awareness (Read Yourself):
I recognize my strengths, weaknesses, drives, and emotions when I interact with others.

Seldom: _____   Sometimes: _____   Usually: _____

Awareness of Others (Read Others/The Room):
I recognize the emotions of others individually and in groups as I interact with them.

Seldom: _____   Sometimes: _____   Usually: _____

Self-Management:
I manage my emotions and behavior and their impact on the emotions, actions, and reactions of others.

Seldom: _____   Sometimes: _____   Usually: _____

Relationship Management
I am able to read the emotions of others and to manage my own emotions and behaviors such that I maximize the effectiveness of my relationships.

Seldom: _____   Sometimes: _____   Usually: _____

Notes:

START
Lead Well • **Be Well** • Do Well

2. Situational Reflection

Best: Contributors

1. Describe a time when your EQ contributed to you responding well to a challenging situation.

2. Consider the factors that may have contributed to your effectiveness.
   - Ample Time
   - Well Prepared
   - Clear Objectives
   - Calm
   - Collaborative
   - Other _____

Stressed: Triggers

1. Describe a time when your lack of EQ contributed to you responding poorly to a challenging situation.

2. Consider the factors that may have triggered your lack of effectiveness.
   - Time Crunched
   - Ill Prepared
   - Lack of Desired Control
   - Unclear Objectives
   - Worried
   - Other _____

3. Taking Action

Identify 2 or 3 things you can do on a consistent basis to support the development of your EQ such that you maximize your Best behavior and minimize your Stressed behavior.

1.

2.

3.

START
Lead Well • Be Well • Do Well

Notes:

Wired: Leadership Styles Summary

Best and Stressed Interacting with others, Complete Leaders are versatile and skilled in the appropriate use of four leadership styles: Command, Coach, Collaborate and Champion. When a leader's behaviors are in sync with what's required in a given situation, they are most effective.

When we're under stress, our leadership styles can be unproductive and can actually interfere with our work and interactions with others. We become more effective both personally and professionally when we maximize times we're at our best, and understand and manage our tendencies when we are stressed.

Reflecting on our leadership styles is the first step in increasing our effectiveness as a complete leader.

Complete Leadership Styles

The Complete Leader: Skilled and experienced in the appropriate use of each style to maximize effectiveness.

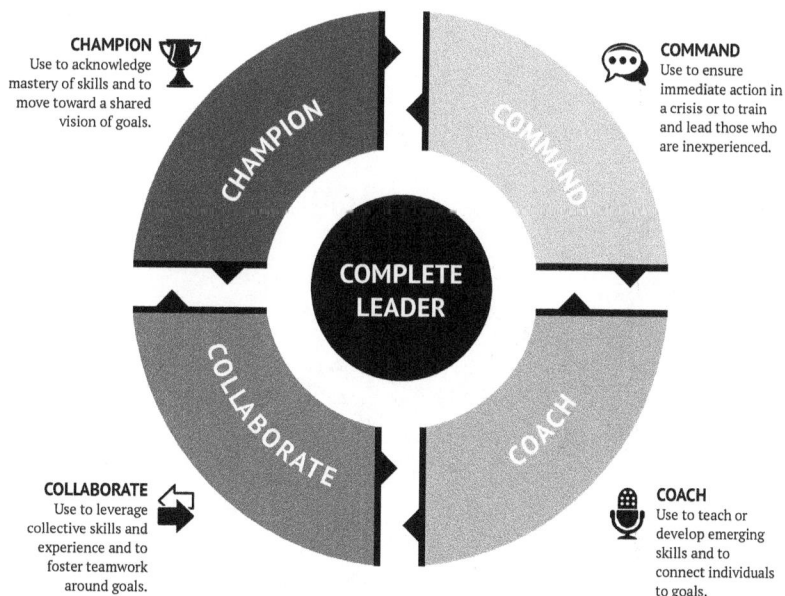

CHAMPION
Use to acknowledge mastery of skills and to move toward a shared vision of goals.

COMMAND
Use to ensure immediate action in a crisis or to train and lead those who are inexperienced.

COMPLETE LEADER

COLLABORATE
Use to leverage collective skills and experience and to foster teamwork around goals.

COACH
Use to teach or develop emerging skills and to connect individuals to goals.

1. Self Reflection

I am familiar with a range of leadership styles and the effect their use has on others.

No: _____   Somewhat: _____   Yes: _____

I use a wide range of leadership styles and match my leadership style to the growing capabilities and circumstances of others.

Seldom: _____   Sometimes: _____   Usually: _____

I am intentional about modeling, teaching, and reinforcing a wide range of leadership styles with others.

Seldom: _____   Sometimes: _____   Usually: _____

I see emerging leadership skills in others that reflect my leadership styles.

Seldom: _____   Sometimes: _____   Usually: _____

Notes:

2. Situational Reflection

Best: Contributors

1. Describe a time you intentionally used a leadership style that was effective in a challenging situation.

2. Consider the factors that may have contributed to your effectiveness.
   - Ample Time
   - Well Prepared
   - Clear Objectives
   - Calm
   - Collaborative
   - Other _____

Stressed: Triggers

1. Describe a time you unintentionally used a leadership style that was not effective in a challenging situation.

2. Consider the factors that may have triggered your lack of effectiveness.
   - Time Crunched
   - Ill Prepared
   - Lack of Desired Control
   - Unclear Objectives
   - Worried
   - Other _____

3. Taking Action

Identify 2 or 3 things you can do to maximize your Best behavior and minimize your Stressed behavior.

1. _____

2. _____

3. _____

START
Lead Well • Be Well • Do Well

Notes:

WIN Map Worksheet

Individual Discovery and Connection

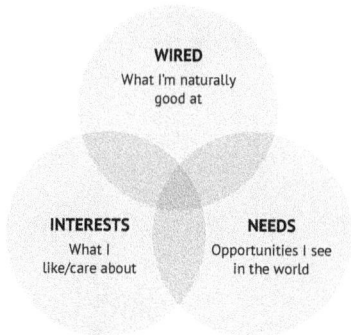

WIRED
What I'm naturally good at

INTERESTS
What I like/care about

NEEDS
Opportunities I see in the world

When you use the way you're innately Wired to address Needs in areas that are of Interest, you engage and excel naturally, creating a greater sense of meaning and success.

Use this WIN Worksheet to assess your strengths and interests and to provide insight over time as you determine a path for meaningful success in addressing needs you see in the world around you. Consider needs you see in family, community, and school/workplace.

W WIRED:
What am I naturally good at?

What comes naturally to me? What are my strengths? When do I feel energized?

_____

_____

_____

_____

_____

_____

_____

_____

I INTERESTS:
What do I like, like to do, and care about?

What subjects do I enjoy? What activities do I like? What do I care about in the world?

_____

_____

_____

_____

_____

_____

_____

_____

N NEEDS:
What opportunities exist for me to contribute?

The world, my community, my work, and my family will benefit from my contribution. What needs do I see?

_____

_____

_____

_____

_____

_____

_____

_____

START
Lead Well • Be Well • Do Well

Notes:

Part Two

Leadership in Action

In this section you'll find the Planning worksheets to guide you in taking the lead in your daily life and in your work using the START Leadership Process. You'll also find a worksheet to guide you in mapping your time (see the Time Map on page 30) and to guide you in taking the lead on projects (see the START Project Process on page 31 and the CREATE Design Thinking Process on page 32).

Using the START Leadership Process,

Strategy serves as a goal-driven, decision-making guide and an organizational framework for you. Identifying your Goals and what you intrinsically Value most serves to inform your Strategy.

Tactics are the activities you select that are instrumental in achieving the Strategy.

Assessments are essential in getting and staying on track to achieving the Strategy.

Routines link daily work to achieving tactics by establishing consistent, repeatable processes.

Training ensures you have identified, developed, and can apply the skills that are necessary to achieve your strategy.

START Leadership Process

STRATEGY	*Strategic vision, values, and goals*
TACTICS	*Tactics to achieve the strategy*
ASSESSMENT	*Assessment to stay on track*
ROUTINES	*Routines link daily work to tactics*
TRAINING	*Training to develop essential skills*

Strategy Worksheet

A Strategy for your life and work, informed by your values, guides your actions and the decisions you make on a daily, monthly, and yearly basis in order to accomplish your long-term goals. Use this worksheet to develop your personal strategy. If you're part of a team, work collaboratively to articulate your team's Strategy in the context of your organization's Strategy.

1. Select Values

Personally, reflect on the attitudes, beliefs, and values you feel are essential to living a successful life, filled with meaning and joy Use the values listed below or on the cards at the end of the workbook to prompt your thinking. Select 4 or 5 core values you feel are most important. Professionally, collaborate with your team to identify the attitudes and values that are essential for doing work that is valued by you, your teammates, and your organization.

Kindness	Integrity	Adventure	Tolerance	Family
Faith	Loyalty	Fun	Courage	Individuality
Hope	Respect	Learning	Work Ethic	_____
Joy	Service	Teamwork	Perseverance	_____

2. Select Goals

Identify and select the 3 or 4 goals that are most important to you/your team.

_____

_____

_____

_____

3. Draft Vision Statement

Draft a short Strategic Vision Statement that reflects these values and goals.

I/we, _____ (insert your name/team) value_____
(list values), and choose activities and actions that support the development of
_____ (list goals), in order to _____
_____ (strategic vision).

Tactics Worksheet

Use your Strategy, WIN Maps, and available Resources—time, attention, and money, as a guide to align and select your Tactical activities. Use the Weekly Time Map on page 30 to gain insight into how your time is currently allocated. If you're part of a team, align the tactical work you're doing as a team with the team's Strategy (strategic vision, values, and goals).

1. List

List all the Tactical activities in which you participate (or want to participate) on Post-It notes—one activity per Post-It. You may choose to separate your personal activities with your work-related activities and complete the Tactical Assessment separately.

2. Align and Implement

Align activities with your Strategy—strategic vision, values, and goals, your WIN Map—Wiring, Interests, and Needs, and with available Resources—time, attention, and money. When selecting Tactics with your team at work, keep in mind that the most effective teams select only 3 to 5 Tactics to work on at one time.

Use the Tactics Decision Tree to facilitate the process.

Tactics Decision Tree

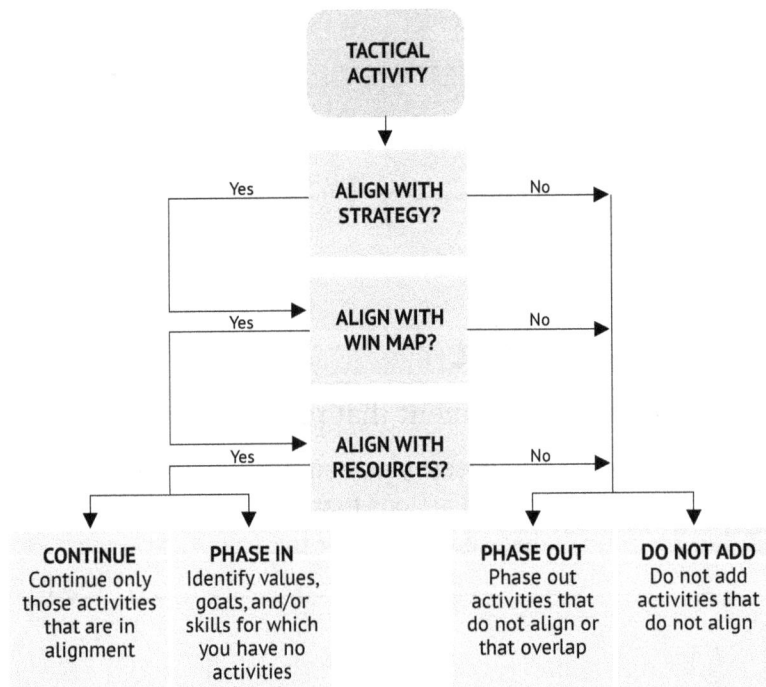

START
Lead Well • Be Well • Do Well

Assessment Worksheet

To stay on track over time, it is important to take time to assess whether or not current activities still align with 1) the values and goals of your Strategy, 2) your WIN maps, and 3) the available resources of time, attention, and money.

1. Schedule

Schedule at least two times during the year to assess alignment.

Date 1	Date 2

2. Align

Using the steps in the Tactics Decision Tree, complete the assessment of activities for you/your team.

Personally

- How well does each activity align with values and goals, wiring and interests, and available resources?
- Develop exit plans to phase out activities that no longer align, and phase in activities that may be missing.

Professionally

- How effective are the selected Tactics proving to be in achieving your Strategy? Have shifting priorities impacted your effectiveness in achieving your Strategy?
- When and where necessary, commit to phasing out Tactical activities that do not align, and to continuing only those that contribute to achieving your Strategy.

3. Acknowledge

Identify areas where your Tactics have aligned to accomplish your/your team's Strategic Goals. Take time to acknowledge and celebrate your success, reflecting on the factors and process you used to you achieve it.

In areas where you have missed the mark, assess the factors that may have contributed and determine how best to revise your approach going forward.

△ **START**
Lead Well • Be Well • Do Well

Routines Worksheet

Use this worksheet for yourself and your team to establish consistent, repeatable processes for the activities you use to accomplish your Tactics. Doing so will allow you to effectively organize the things you do on a daily, weekly, or monthly basis, creating capacity to deal with inevitable challenges that arise in work and life. Routines establish a path to efficiently achieve your strategic goals.

1. Assess

Assess each of your activities and the ways they align to support the achievement of your Tactics. Take your personal habits and the existing patterns of interaction between you and your team members into consideration—noting where they support success and where they may interfere.

2. Establish Routines

Establish Routines (processes) for all the things you do on a daily, weekly, or monthly basis in your personal life, in your work, and on your team.
- Identify the activities required to complete your selected Tactics
  - Personally: Include routines for morning, lunch time, evening, exercise, down time, sleep, etc
  - Professionally: Include meeting, reports, updates, work products, etc.
- Break the activities down into their elemental components
- Establish a set of repeatable steps into a workable routine you can use to minimize their variance and maximize their efficiency, effectiveness, and consistency.

3. Take Action

Assume responsibility for putting routines into practice:
- Implement one routine at a time to ensure effectiveness. Modify as necessary.
- Practice until the routines become habit (approximately 21 days).
- Notice and address challenges or issues that may threaten implementation.

Training Worksheet

According to Business and Academic Leaders today, 10 categories of skills are essential for you to lead well, be well, and do well in the 21st Century. These skills are listed and defined on the following page. Use this worksheet to assess, track, and develop these skills over time.

1. Assess Skills

Now and periodically over time, assess the extent to which you have developed and mastered each skill. Note in the space next to each skill which are D: Developing or M: Mastered.

2. Track Skill Development

Document the assessments you make with respect to skills so that you can track improvement or spot areas for development over time.

Date _____

1. _____ Global Awareness
2. _____ Ethics
3. _____ Self Direction
4. _____ Grit
5. _____ EQ
6. _____ Social Responsibility
7. _____ Critical Thinking
8. _____ Creativity
9. _____ Communication
10. _____ Collaboration

3. Create Development Opportunities

Take action to create opportunities and participate in activities that allow you to learn, practice, develop, and master each of these skills over time.

Reflect on the progress you're making. Take on increasingly challenging opportunities that will build your capabilities as you develop more sophisticated aspects of each skill.

START
Lead Well • Be Well • Do Well

10 Essential Leadership Skills

Responsible

1. **Global Awareness** I understand the perspective of others who may have needs and views that are different from my own.

2. **Ethics** I choose right over wrong—even when choosing right is harder and no one is watching.

3. **Self-Direction** I see the big picture. I set appropriate goals, and I take initiative and ownership to do the work necessary to achieve them.

Resilient

4. **Grit** I recover from setbacks, and I forge ahead. I am willing, eager, and able to take on worthwhile challenges even when it is hard.

5. **EQ** I have the social and emotional skills that enable me to effectively manage myself and my relationships.

6. **Social Responsibility** I put my talents to work to make a difference in ways that are meaningful to my community and to me.

Resourceful

7. **Critical Thinking** I have the knowledge, skill, and discipline to conceptualize, analyze, and synthesize information that leads to meaningful and productive decision making.

8. **Creativity** I have the knowledge, skill, and discipline to apply original ideas to generate meaningful value.

9. **Communication** I persuasively give and actively receive essential information.

10. **Collaboration** I work with and leverage a group's talents to realize shared goals.

START
Lead Well • Be Well • Do Well

Time Map
24 Hours / Day

Directions   In the chart (page 30), each box represents an hour of time in your day, organized in eight-hour blocks, for each day of the week.

- Using *black*, color in a block for each hour you spend at work, doing work, or completing other obligations.

- Using *blue*, color in a block for each hour you spend sleeping.

- In the remaining unscheduled hours, use *green* to color in a block for each hour you typically spend reflecting, thinking, dreaming, creating, reading, resting, relaxing, connecting with family, spending time in nature, listening to music, enjoying the arts, etc.

- Using *yellow*, color in a block for each hour you typically spend connecting in person with friends.

- Using *orange*, color in a block for each hour you typically spend watching TV, playing video games, on social media, etc.

Reflect   Notice the number of hours you have each day for free time and for sleep during the week and on weekends.

- You need 7–8 hours of sleep per night to support memory, mood, and performance. Are you getting that?

- Notice the amount of free time you have and how you are spending it. Does it feel like you have enough unscheduled time to relax and decompress, to be creative, to connect, to rest, to dream?

- If you have less free time than you'd like, what might you do to create more free time or down time each day? Are there things you could eliminate or consolidate? Are there ways you can be more efficient on certain tasks? Can you identify areas of interest where you would enjoy spending time?

Take Action   Assess the way you're spending your time, and look for opportunities to optimize your schedule over time. Use the Tactics Worksheet to align and prioritize the activities you select to continue or add and those you select to phase in or out.

Time Map
24 Hours / Day

Monday

8 am – 5 pm							
5 pm – 11 pm							
11 pm – 8 am							

Tuesday

8 am – 5 pm							
5 pm – 11 pm							
11 pm – 8 am							

Wednesday

8 am – 5 pm							
5 pm – 11 pm							
11 pm – 8 am							

Thursday

8 am – 5 pm							
5 pm – 11 pm							
11 pm – 8 am							

Friday

8 am – 5 pm							
5 pm – 11 pm							
11 pm – 8 am							

Saturday

8 am – 5 pm							
5 pm – 11 pm							
11 pm – 8 am							

Sunday

8 am – 5 pm							
5 pm – 11 pm							
11 pm – 8 am							

Use this Project Process worksheet to guide you in taking the lead on projects. Use the CREATE Innovation Process (page 32) to first identify the Need you/your team are seeking to address.

START Project Process

STRATEGY	*What are our Project Goals?*
TACTICS	*What will we do to achieve them?*
ASSESSMENT	*Who will do what?*
RESOURCES	*What will we need to complete it?*
TIMELINE	*When will it be complete?*

Use this Innovation Process worksheet to assess a Need that is of Interest to you/ your organization. Then use the START Project Process (page 31) to clarify your goals and plan how you'll accomplish them.

CREATE Innovation Process

C	*Connect to community to identify a need*
R	*Refine the need*
E	*Explore possible solutions to address it*
A	*Agree on one*
T	*Try it*
E	*Evaluate, and if necessary, repeat*

CONCLUSION

Lead Well, Be Well, Do Well

START provides the tools you need to take the lead in your life—personally and professionally. When you put the processes to work over time, they will provide a path to greater well being, happiness, and meaningful success.

Developing and mastering the skills you need to maximize opportunities—while navigating the inevitable challenges you'll face—is an ongoing process. Now and at each new phase of your life, using these tools will serve you well in mapping a path that is both productive and fulfilling.

START provides a map to Lead Well, Be Well, and Do Well in the life you make for yourself.

Live Well.

BIBLIOGRAPHY

Research in Business

Emotional Intelligence by Daniel Goleman
Peter Drucker on the Profession of Management by Peter Drucker
Gallup StrengthsFinder 2.0 by Tom Rath
Good to Great by Jim Collins
The Happiness Advantage by Shawn Achor
Scaling Up Excellence by Bob Sutton and Huggy Rao
A Whole New Mind by Daniel Pink
Creative Confidence by Tom and David Kelley
Mindset by Carol Dwek
Work Rules by Laszlo Bock

Wiring Resource Links

Gallup Organization: www.gallupstrengthscenter.com
Myers Briggs: www.myersbriggs.org

Books in the START Series

START: Lead Well, Do Well, Be Well
Equip your kids with the mindset and skills they need to thrive in a highly competitive world

START Family Workbook: Lead Well, Do Well, Be Well
Equip your kids with the mindset and skills they need to thrive in a highly competitive world

START Student Workbook: Lead Well, Do Well, Be Well
Develop the mindset and skills you need take the lead in a highly competitive world

Values Selection

A card deck may be a useful tool when discussing and selecting your personal values. The values and definitions provided on the following pages can be used to inform your decision. Use the blanks to include additional values you consider to be important.

You may also want to consider doing this exercise with your team, to establish a set of team values. If you do, consider inviting everyone to identify their top 5 values using Post-It flags or initials. The 5 values that receive the most votes can serve to enhance the connection team members feel towards one another and towards the collective team.

There are no right or wrong answers. The process of considering, choosing, and living according to a set of values that resonate for you/your team has been proven over time to drive superior outcomes.

VALUES

······

Integrity

······

VALUES

······

Joy

······

VALUES

······

Hope

······

VALUES

······

Faith

······

VALUES

······

Kindness

······

VALUES

······

Fun

······

VALUES

······

Adventure

······

VALUES

······

Service

······

VALUES

······

Respect

······

VALUES

······

Loyalty

······

Integrity
Example: We are honest and tell the truth, and in so doing, we earn each other's trust.

Fun
Example: We celebrate our wins, use respectful humor, and find time to play.

Joy
Example: By connecting to what we value most, we maintain a sense of well being that is independent of immediate circumstance.

Adventure
Example: We enjoy discovering and participating in new experiences and activities.

Hope
Example: We are optimistic that when we work towards meaningful goals, things will get better.

Service
Example: Contributing to the good of others even when it does not directly benefit us is important and gives us a greater sense of purpose.

Faith
Example: We believe in something bigger than ourselves.

Respect
Example: We treat others as intelligent, capable, and worthy of our time and attention.

Kindness
Example: We are nice, compassionate, and patient with each other; we speak respectfully and listen carefully; we take turns, and cooperate.

Loyalty
Example: We value close relationships, make significant effort to maintain those connections, and support those close to us when necessary.

VALUES	VALUES
Work Ethic	
Courage	
Tolerance	**Individuality**
Teamwork	**Family**
Learning	**Perseverance**

Work Ethic
Example: We take initiative, work hard, and are reliable and diligent. We do challenging work we know is important.

Courage
Example: We have confidence to try new things, are not afraid to make mistakes, and have strength to continue even when times are challenging.

Tolerance
Example: We value and respect the contributions and differences between members of our family, school, community, and world.

Teamwork
Example: We work cooperatively and put the work and outcomes of the team ahead of ourselves individually.

Learning
Example: We believe in being curious and creative and believe it is important to expand our knowledge and sharpen our skills in advisory and throughout our lifetime.

Individuality
Example: We value the characteristics and attributes that make each of us unique, even though differences can sometimes make it challenging for us to get along.

Family
Example: We value our time together as a family. Doing family activities or having meals together is as important as individual activities.

Perseverance
Example: We commit to doing our best to learn and to achieve important goals, and we stick with it, even when it is hard.

Notes

Notes

Notes